*For my sister,*
*whose unconditional love is inspiring!*

# Table of Contents

You and I are close… "friends." Fortunes favor us as we bask in the pretense of our own cerebral nakedness. Everything about US compliments a thought of "us" yet everything about "us" is wrong.          An inner confrontation of wrong and not so wrong; of incorrect yet          mathematically we lose nothing by taking a chance.

Friendship, well defined as a                    relationship regarded with liking,                    affection and loyalty. Pictures are painted about          the thought. Music is sung, movies are made, poems are written. Yet,          crossing the line always has a happy ending. What do we lose? Nothing.          Our          memories exchange wishes abundantly wrapped in          smiles, tears, strength and laughter. Our hands          clammer in sweat holding each other when the          sun          goes down and appears to have been lost in the          night.          Our bodies touch creating a physical reaction          suprising          us both as we bear the thought of "us".

Our          movies pan                    the same genres. Our songs     intertwine                    with the                    times of classics. Our books plot narratives of historical          tales, fictional characters and mystical magicians. Our hobbies require quiet and sensory affection; complimented by the sounds of waves and rain. Yet, this poem, is about friendship. Not love. And yet, still about love.

1

## SHE...

scares me.  Shakes

the   very ground I walk on.  Trembles the

earth whose foundation is fortressed by cement.  She

touches me... without touching me. My skin erodes as we

breathe the same air in the same space.  She rekindles the flame

doused by past experiences, I want the spark. A moment not

yet conceived or brought to life but my mind has preconceived

thoughts about her. Why is she so new to me yet I've known

her for so long? I want to explore the very crevices of her

thoughts.  Travel the undulating tides of her fantasies.

Remove her stress by caressing the tensed covers of

her soul.  Reintroduce myself to her as if we'd

never exchanged names before.  Hi,

my name, is… Is she opposed to

conversing?

2

If so,

then please let me gift wrap

this compliment and move on, but while we are

sitting in this place at this time, let's write a poem together.

Compose a few stanzas that embrace affection yet comfortably

disclose our thoughts.  Give clarity to our intentions as I do not wish to

have an intimate moment with her, I wish to share an intimate lifetime!

What are her dreams? I'd like to be a part of them.  What are her

thoughts? I'd like to exchange the very best of ourselves.  What are

her aspirations? I'd like to support them.  She does not complete

me, for only God can do that, but she makes me feel good,

like a man, a good man. She gives me confidence, an

extra strut in my walk. She makes me want to make

her breakfast (yes, breakfast)!  Hi, my name

is ... as she opened her eyes, Good

morning.

3

Mental note, don't rush this. I'm sitting on the cuspice of moving too fast and just because the mind thinks it's OK, doesn't mean its OK to ask. Slow down... while embracing this beauty, you could also be pushing her away. Preparing her for something that she is not prepared for but a man needs to be aggressive, this is the war. I'm impatient to embrace her as mine but past conversations create resistance... Yet innuendos and inference gives the mind a split second in time to think this: our friendship is immovable, but this jones... this jones... it is not an infatuation, it's an inkling. A passionate interest... something that tells me that our mathematics creates formulas to perfect equations. A hypothesis yet proven stating that our elements create amazing electron configurations. And though I may feel like I know her, I still want to delve into the shelves of her mind to acquire more information. So I'm patient. But as slow as I'd like to move, I still want to groove to the rhythm of her heart. Why the resistance? I'm still trying to understand her situation, so I humble myself.

Fortunes amassed in the corners my mind,

I am wealthy beyond human measurement yet poor.

Her name is engraved in my vellum,

a brown parchment which is my skin

and she has written her very existence into me.

She calls me friend and I call her love.

A not so secret attraction hidden behind complex affections.

A life of rhythm, my mind sings endless acapellas of her beauty.

I have found her name in the examples of that definition,

We share 8 hours of uninterrupted harmony; she is the subject of my dreams.

My body yearns for her, misses her

Yet we have never shared the pleasurable afflictions of making love.

# Love Lost in Likes

Held safely in her bosom I decided to write these stanzas.
Caressing her face like painting perfection on canvas.
Lost in her multiple choices, I decided to search for answers
to the simple questions of our lives.

Why do you love me?
From within me there is a need, (better yet) an intention
to define like as a constant search for love
and though I love you, I like you 100 times greater.
As long as I like you you will continue to melt in my mouth like Life Savers.
You are my life saver; the center of my being like meridians and equators.
I pretend love has eluded me simply because when love is lost...
like just likes to search for her...
and I like to search for her.

This woman breathes life into my equations.
She creates permeating sensations from each brain cortex.
I like her so much I'd scale the walls of her fortress
just to witness the wonders of her thoughts.
When she is distraught, I am inclined to write rhymes and stanzas
not to provide answers but to give her a moment.

Why do I like you?
Because your voice squeaks when your happy.
Your smile gives life to the world around you.
Your skin is soft as velvet and your style is misjudged by swag.
Because you realize that the world is not molded by what we've had or what we have

You are truth and I like that.
You make me want to sing songs about liking you
But no song is as great as actually liking loving you!

# 09

## DREAMS

I've learned that love wraps itself around faith and clinches it's wings to the soul.

Life itself is poor without this one thing:
unrequited, uncontrolled love.
We sustain moments and wish for miracles
but we only pray when the ship is sinking.
Falsified lover, my life changes with a jolt or a slight inkling
I'm thinking that simple can be so complex
yet being difficult is so easy.
For a smile, love loses to embarrassment
because the best memories are kind of cheesy.
Pants ripping on the first date
or dropping buffalo chicken sauce on a white t-shirt,
sometimes simply saying that "you look great" is good enough.
Fluff lines removed and conversation becomes simple.

Our likes and dislikes placed on the table like dessert.
Sweet to savor honesty like vanilla ice cream with a soft-baked foundation.
Low maintenance with high expectations, could I smile more?

"What are you searching for?" She asked.
A simple yet complex question.
A lack of response exudes a lack of confidence yet the maticulous nature of a list cre-
ates a perception that I will not bend.
I simply responded:
"I am searching for a friend but even greater,
I am searching for inspiration to write again."

Her heartbeat, the
metronome to my living.
Our skins touch and my
physical reaction hints to
my thinking.
Devastated thoughts
dormant like wishing.

*Simple seduction without kissing.*

12

## Blue Bed Time Stories

Fortune strokes the lips
as this temptress alludes to the very pleasures I long for.
I dream of us intertwined in the very essence of love-making.
Romance, a self loathing noun cordially convinced
that affection will become its verb, an action only shared between two,
yet the result is a singularity.
We taste the very nipples of love yet love lay unpleased.
She is the very essence of what brings men to their knees.
Teased to an extended degree without an inkling of pleasure.
Testicles matching the skies on a cloudless day
And even still… I can only think of her beauty as we lay.
As we lay we share stories:
All of the things the ex never did,
future fortunes that have yet to come true,
all of the crazy things she's done or wish to do
and if I lean in for a kiss,
Brick.

She's not ready: hell bent on using her past as an excuse.
Then a light bulb: *I can't touch her.*
And as much as I may want to, I can't love her.
In her mind, the ex's hands still caress her skin,
she still reminisces about her nights with him
and she wants now what she had then
before the fights, arguments and adulterous sin…

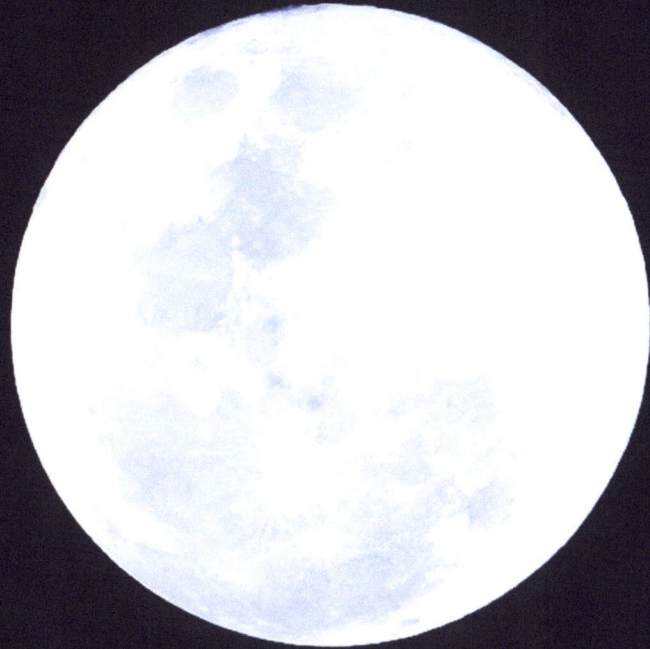

I can't love her!
As much as she thinks she
has opened up,
it doesn't mean that she
has let me in.

I put it in... slowly... naturally... raw.
I funneled my shovel deep into her buried treasure.
A finite feeling with infinite measure.
Awaiting the crippling sensation, highlighted punctuation with an exclamation of extreme pleasure.
The war to see who was better, this sinful fornication with oils and feathers.
We'd only known each other for a few weeks before we decided to lay together.
No discussions of whether or not we would stay together:
intentions vague; I barely knew her.

Her hobbies were mysteries supplanted into an abyss of uncommon secrets.
Though my lips touched her skin in incremental spaces.
Running my fingers across her back as her heart races.
Artistically creating visions in the dark as my hand mimics artistic traces.
Whispers and breathing: pleasure writes stanzas across our faces.

Wrecklessness sparked by the removal of her red dress
The instance of "us" physical in nature: attraction based on innuendos pictured from the neck down.
I became an addict to her melanin, a fiend to her touch
A slave to her requests.

I shared me sparingly and later, it became clear to me that I was more scared of commitment than getting HIV.

I
fumigate fictional fallacies,
formidable opponent of the forbidden.  I
hustle because my past is centered around instability; a
future laid in the cement of tranquility.  A veracious lapse in
time that time has forgotten… I have forgotten how to love you in
exchange for remembering how to love myself. An inheritance of wealth
greater than pirates gold on an oceanic shelf.  My love for myself is Scrooge
McDuck money and even though        I accept that we all have to struggle,
it was my dad who taught me
how to hustle.  Goal-setting
genetic implantation.  "I will
be successful" focus meditation
incantation.  I send prayers
to God hoping he sends me
something back with overnight
delivery.  I don't ask for favors, I ask
for signs. However, I understand he may
not come when I call… But he's always on time!
My life is sweet haven wrapped in
sensations of virility.
A new chapter of
my life written
with auspicious
tranquility.

*I am happy!*
*What are you?*

*the Question*

There is a moment,
a small instance of time that will last forever.
No other minute is as dear,
no other second is as precious,
no other hour is as beautiful.
This moment.
Where the laws of science are broken as two become one.
Where a dream deferred through chronology is no longer on pause.
A moment where the sun shines through the rain and the wind settles.
Where dew drops lay rest on the pedals of roses
and a full moon refuses to rise the high tide.
Let this moment be yours.

We are all witnesses to this promissory note written in passion and affection.
To this reserved space where your love embraces the dawn of a new day.
We have all been witnesses to the story written into the parchment of time.
Where two strangers became friends, two friends became partners and today, two partners:
soul mates.
The journey has just begun.
The destination, unknown.
The path is no golden brick road but in your best of times, and your worst of times
remember:
the sun will always rise to the dawn of a new day.
The moon will forever share its beauty with the stars of the night sky.
The grass will grow, the trees will age and this moment, will last forever!

Dedicated to Juan & Shannon Rios

Hearts broken at the end of sentences
Manhood removed on the other side of a phone call
"I hate you."
Screamed at the top of her lungs to a dial tone.
A glass is broken, thrown from the other side of the room.
A table is flipped and anger has found herself a new home.
Revenge written into the mind like a Tolkien adventure:
there is no ring.
With everything invested, there was no ring.
She wanted a ring.

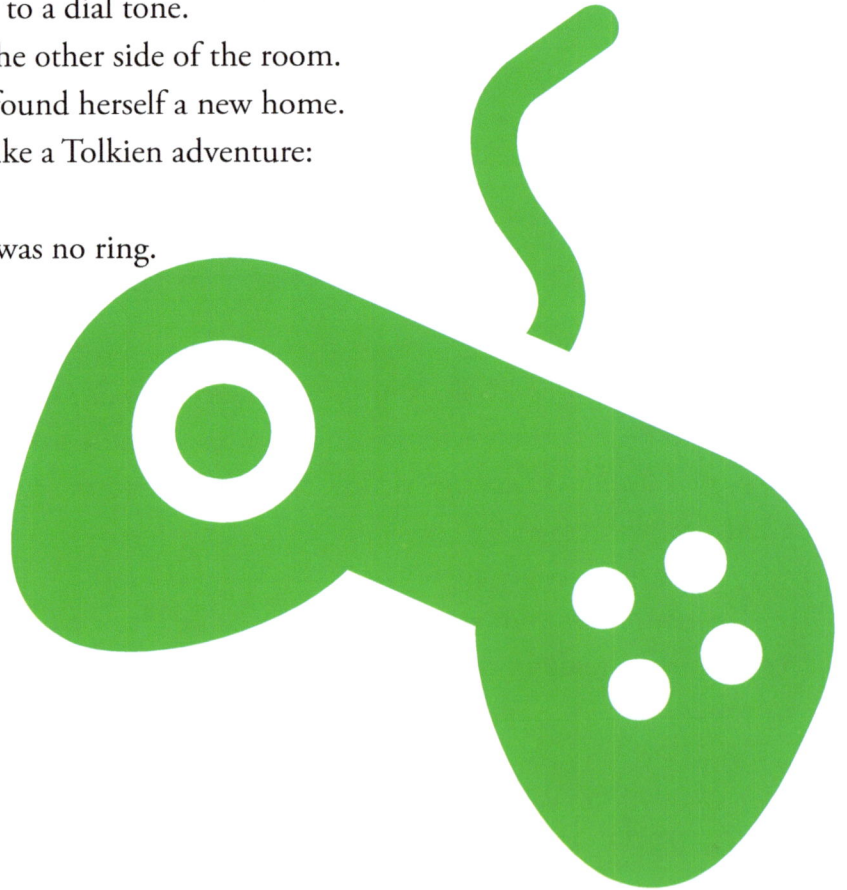

The American dream is not so American to her anymore.
The thought of a house and children allude her.
Each day increases her age,
each moment raises her wisdom.

She settled and she knew it.

He was lost in her shape, found solace in her lips
and satisfaction between her hips.
Her wallet was attractive but he was still a boy.
Playgrounds and video games are a boy's best friend
and she didn't like playing games.
Even in wisdom she let him in
And he hooked up his Xbox.
She said, "I love you."
He said, "Me too."
She said, "Let's go away."
He said, "Let's just hang out at home."
She said, "When are we getting married."
He said, "Let's just hang out at home."

Hang out at home.

The break up.
Hearts broken at the end of sentences.
Manhood removed on the other side of a phone call.
"I hate you," she screamed at the top of her lungs to a dial tone.

Too many questions.
Statements made with uncertainty.
Doctrines decreed yet answers are few.
Inquiries answered with quandaries.
And the weary tell tales of tire.
Liar, culprit of innocent thoughts turned guilty.
Friendly, clean thoughts turned filthy.
You have the skill to comfort me but you are not with me.
All I have are these stories: memories.
"The good ole days".
A time before our time became the time we ran away from.
Kryptonite, everything time forgot
because it was everything time wanted me to stay away from. Elation
died with our love, what'd you expect?
At some point we exchanged making love for sex.

King of the jungle,
but lions don't sleep
with lambs.
I became a lamb.

Hopeless.

I've contemplated the subject for most of my recent existence

and the thought takes hold of my interests leaving my body numb to the senses.

Unfocused lenses, it's become so predictable that even my thoughts can predict the end of a thoughts sentence.

I guess this is my sentence for hearts broken without apology.

The love letters torn into pieces; lost for so long that being lost becomes the lie that the lie is believing.

Achievements mask the lack thereof.

Covering the true monster inside but if the glove fits, you're guilty!


Beguiled into believing that you may get one, sometimes two.

I had one and I still remember her.

Her skin gave beauty to the scientific thought of melanin.

A year of convincing, she let me in after shutting the door to so many.

I loved her, she accepted my shortcomings.

We made love like love making knew nothing.

The passion brought me to my knees as we produced orgasmic reactions from simple touching.

The room was small, the bed uncomfortable yet the covers seemed to always fit.
She kissed my neck and it gave me chills.
I remember her, she held me until I couldn't cry anymore.
Until my skin permeated the smell of her perfume and our oils made love potions and we inhaled the fumes of each other.
I had found my best friend, it just so happens she was also a compatible lover.
And I loved her.

Truthful in her approach this woman knew me.
Falsified emotions could not be covered, she saw through me.
She would kiss me and reassure me that things would be alright.
Sometimes that meant that she needed to stay up all night but she didn't mind, our lives were alternating verses and she could finish my lines.
It's true, love is blind.

A greater part of her misfortune, she didn't want to believe
I left… she fought for me to stay but in the fray
She was a victim of my drunken sobriety.
She'll never forgive me,
And why should she?
I loved her, but what more: she loved me.

At the beginning, she didn't see me coming, but in the end, she didn't see me leave!

Sanity, quiet contemporary concoction filled with fresh perspective like sobriety, two shots and you're back where you started. Dazed and confused, self inflicted pain sustained without treatment: heartache.

Band-aids covering each suicidal thought like jackets in cold winters and love makes you run into a snow storm half naked. Trinkets with sentimental value burned in the stockpile of memories: you just want to forget and you lose it. Shivering in a corner of self pity trusting nothing of your senses; knuckles bleeding and fists still clenched.

A hug is no comfort while you smash furniture and burn birthday cards on the furnace of an electric stove. "Fuck you" written on white walls with spray paint filling an insatiable appetite for misery.

And you struggle. Sanity eludes capture and frustration sings melodies of House of Pain and Marylin Manson. It ends when it ends, in the mean time, lip sync something angry and flip the bird.

Time tells stories. Silly little moments shift into memories that I can't forget. Simply shifting focus yet the melody of this song is more beautiful than that of any opus tho the orchestra has lost it's tune. The trumpeter is consumed because he can no longer find the right pitch. The drummer has lost his rhythm and playing no longer soothes the soul. The trombone hasn't found a home in the brass section and the woodwinds haven't sat down. Violas and violins are still being strung and the conductor is ready to play.

But there is no orchestra.

The very nature of his job is lost in things he cannot control. All he wants to do is play music, 8 bars at a time. The second step of the G-clef where clarinets and strings surprise most by sharing notes that only they can play. The cornet calls the brass it's home and lays down history as it belts history and the sound is so soothing.

It's all in his head.

The perfect key, the perfect melody.  It all feels so right until the lead gets sick and keys are out of tune.

The ride is an undulating roller coaster of lower C's and warm ups.  The moments are pissed to the wind like high notes in a snow storm.  And the uneducated listeners in the concert hall judge.

Everyone has an opinion.

The competing conductors slam him for an embarrassing performance and they celebrate the victory.  He walks away wondering what if the music was too high or if the saxophonist wasn't sick?  What if the flutes were in sync and xylophone wasn't missing a key?

In the end, a new song was played, Regardless of how it sounded, the tune touched the very ear drums of heaven.

For that, there is a reason to be thankful!

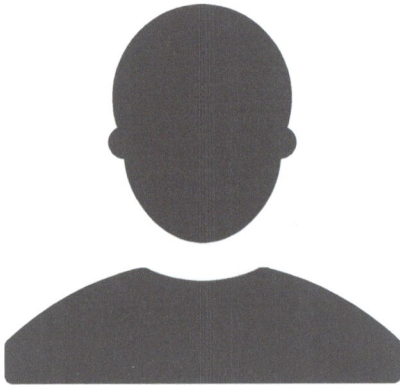

| | |
|---|---|
| Description | Single Black Male. |
| Status | Never married. |
| Children | No children (though I hope to have some some day). |
| Height | 5' maybe 9" |
| Summary | Spoken word, design and changing the world are my interests. |

I rely on my 5 senses and I'm from the now generation so I have a limited amount of patience.

So rather than keep you waiting, I'll get to the point of what I'm saying... I HATE online dating.

Profile #1 **Shaniqua145:** She had pretentious descriptions and inscriptions written on her profile page. Biological clock was ticking but I'm thinking this was just a phase. Her favorite quote: "I'm paid" cited from a rap song she heard the other day. "Miss Independent" is what she claimed forgetting to mention that she still needed mom and dad for a place to stay. But its OK, I'm on to the next one (I guess I'll quote Jay).

Profile #2 **Bonqueisha:** She professed to like old school and classic movies (I'm still trying to figure out what she meant). She logged on with one specific intent: Soul mate search. Standards lowered in an effort to not scare anyone away, yet her profile read: In search of a serious relationship; not here for the games *(chess move 101)*. So I skipped her just to be safe.

Profile #3 **Unexpected3:** 5'5", single and slim is how she described her waist. Profile pictures were gorgeous though never questioned if they were real or fake. I live in Connecticut and she was a little out of state but that was OK. We conversed for a few weeks before deciding to schedule a first date. We'd meet at a cafe.

Walked in...

Me: "A young lady is expecting me"

Hostess: "Yes sir, let me show you to her table"

"Here you are sir"

She looked up and smiled. I ordered a few drinks.

Unexpected3: "What do you think?" I ordered more drinks.

"This has been really nice, so will you call me?"

Me: "Maybe."

Her profile pictures were dated illusions taken years prior. Her interests changed like a crescendoing song. Maybe it's the sites that I am on. Maybe online dating is just wrong. All thoughts running through my head as I sign up for Match.com.

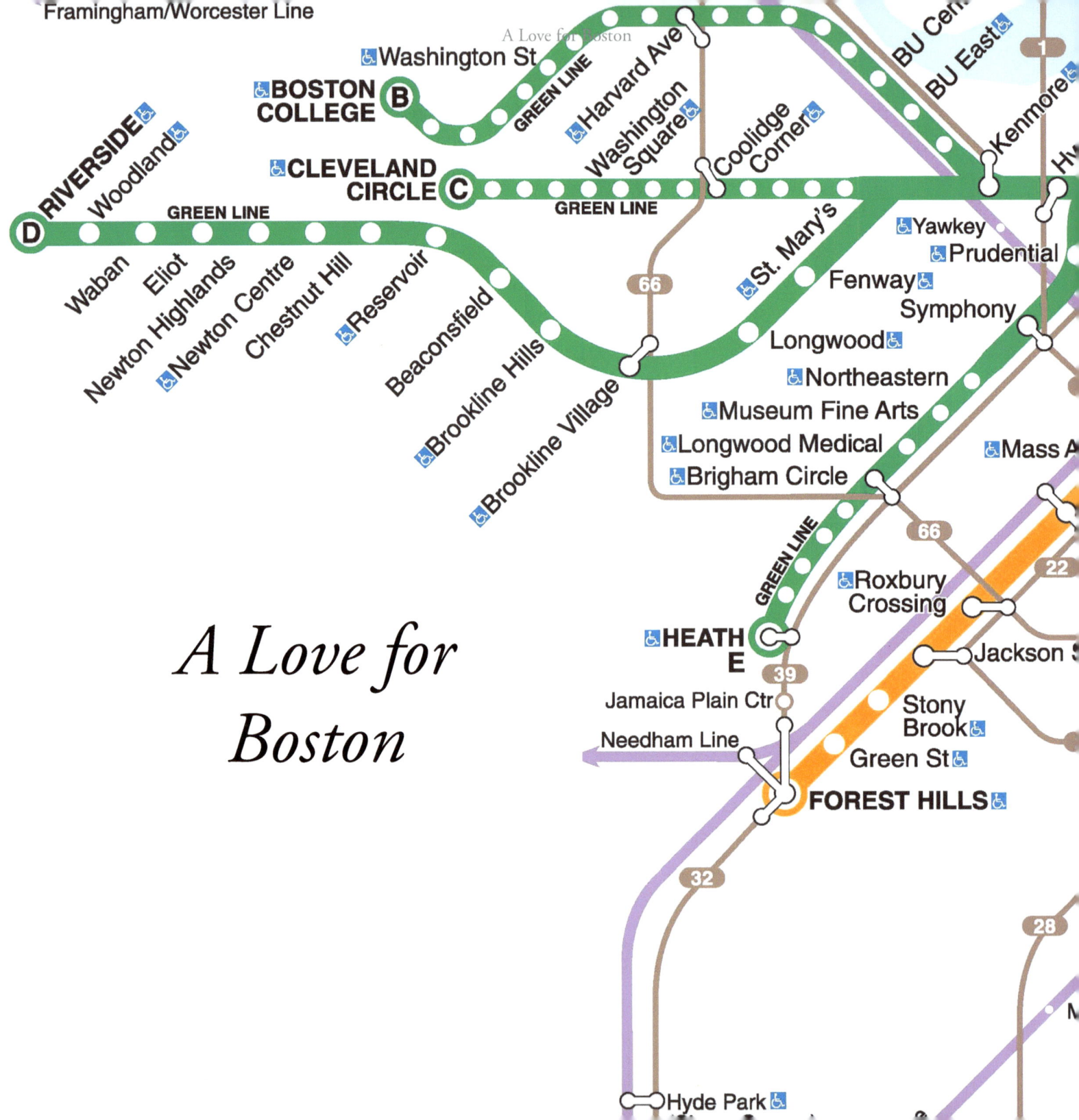

Framingham/Worcester Line

Washington St

**BOSTON COLLEGE** (B)

**CLEVELAND CIRCLE** (C)

GREEN LINE

Harvard Ave

Washington Square

Coolidge Corner

GREEN LINE

GREEN LINE

(D) **RIVERSIDE**

Woodland

Waban

Eliot

Newton Highlands

Newton Centre

Chestnut Hill

Reservoir

Beaconsfield

Brookline Hills

Brookline Village

66

St. Mary's

BU Cen

BU East

Kenmore

1

Yawkey

Prudential

Fenway

Symphony

Longwood

Northeastern

Museum Fine Arts

Longwood Medical

Brigham Circle

Mass A

66

GREEN LINE

*A Love for*

*Boston*

**HEATH** E

Jamaica Plain Ctr

Needham Line

39

Roxbury Crossing

Jackson

Stony Brook

Green St

**FOREST HILLS**

22

32

28

Hyde Park

Center

Aquarium

*State

Arlington

Park St

Logan Ferry Terminal

Logan International Airport

Long Wharf South

Rowes Wharf

Downtown Crossing

Boylston

Courthouse

World Trade Ctr

Silver Line Way

SL5

SL4

SL1

F1   F2

Chinatown

SILVER LINE SL1 & SL2

SL2

DESIGN CENTER

Back Bay

Tufts Medical

South Station

F2H

To Hull

To Hingham

Herald St

SILVER LINE SL4 & SL5

E. Berkeley St

Union Park St

Broadway

Newton St

Worcester Sq

SILVER LINE SL4 & SL5

Mass Ave

Boston Medical Center

Andrew

Lenox St

Melnea Cass

F2

DUDLEY SQ

JFK/UMass

23

Uphams Corner

28

15

Kane Square

Hall

22

RED LINE

28

Savin Hill

22

23

Fields Corner

Codman Square

RED LINE

22

Shawmut

North Quincy

23

ASHMONT

Wollaston

"It's certainly nice to see you, wow, you look great."

Words exchanged at first glance short stops the brain to take an extra second to observe. Innate response seemed inappropriate so I took the chance to stop and find the words. Clearly I was mistaken, shaken in my realization that nothing had changed, you were still very much the same but it's amazing how different you seemed.

I simply wanted to be close to you, create a physical connection so we hugged and though the next few hours were ours together, I didn't want to let go. As we sat on the train, I wanted our shoulders to touch. When the waitress delivered our drinks, I reached over to feel your energy.
We clashed on the way back from the restroom flashing a smile.

I was happy, happier than I'd been in a long time. Maybe it was because I had not seen you in a long time but a long time created long times where all I wanted was to stare for long times. We took the T home. Green line. We were just hanging out, catching up, but it almost felt like we were the only ones on the train. No one else. Maybe I was tired, but I couldn't help but stare.

We separated. I caught cab to scour the city for my towed car. How about coffee tomorrow?

Goodnight.

# Fickle,

Selfish solution to a situation not
labeled as a problem.
Funny that I find solitude to be so
befitting when all I want is freedom.
Individual independence initiated by a
sense of selfishness.
Healing the heart at its own pace, in its
own time, its own space.
But the confession remains apparent:
I am not ready!

Dear Mom,

With your permission, I'd like to give you a lesson on air,
and yes, you heard that correctly, air.
From the dawn of time, there are some things that have never been taught.
Things that we can instantly do from the moment we step out of the womb.
We can look, we can smile, we can cry, we can breathe
Breathing, an innate function given to us from God and therefore only He can take it
away.
A forgettable requirement on the road of life, it sustains us.

Without it, we are nothing.

Scientists explore it to see if there is a way to replicate it, they cannot.
Astronauts explore other planets, in hopes of finding it, they have not.
Environmentalists attempt to test it to see if they can purify it, they have yet to do so.
No one understands it, yet, we live. And it is the one thing we cannot live without.
Life is permeated by it, the clouds use it to produce rain, the water vaporizes it to produce
clouds, the sun pierces it to produce heat and something so important tends to be
forgotten in the midst of our living.

So I've written this piece for you.
So that you know I have not forgotten.
You are my air.  Your very embrace gives me life.
Your very existence gives me purpose.
Your affectionate love gives me warmth.
If time could stand still it should stop at this very moment.
The moment that I script a letter, set it to a flame and let it drift into the wind as I tell that which gave me life, that it is appreciated. Mommy, you are appreciated.
For the moments of wisdom, the moments of discipline, the shoulder to cry on, the wall to hold me, the vehicle to get me home, the voice to let me sleep, the support to keep me pushing, the air to keep me breathing.

This is for you.

Our love is not lost in translation,
it isn't a note washed away as a message in a bottle,
it isn't forgotten as the brain wears away.
It is the very essence of who I am.

And as you have given me life,
I promise you, I will save a breathe for you.

Milton Jackson is a Hartford, Connecticut based poet and member of the spoken word group, Poetry to the People.  Poetically known as Rahnik, Milton has been performing since 1997, joined with Kendall Exume in 2002 and has since performed at over 100 venues across the United States.

Milton has published other anthologies including *Life, Liberty & Love, Fire Light: Some Kind of Wonderful, Freedom: Next Exit* and *Defying Gravity: I Was Chosen* (co-authored by Kendall Exume).

For more information, visit www.poetrytothepeople.com

www.ingramcontent.com/pod-product-compliance
Lightning Source LLC
Chambersburg PA
CBHW042100040426